MW01264916

Miscarriages

My Story

By Kathleen Smith

Copyright © 2011, 2014 by Kathleen Smith

All rights reserved.

Printed in the United States of America

978-1500710040

Subject Heading: RELIGION / Christian Life /
Women's Issues

Scripture quotations are from the King James
Version (KJV). Public Domain

Cover art based on the photography of E Dina
PhotoArt

Dedication

I would like to dedicate this book to my husband for all the love and support he has given to me throughout the time it took me in writing this book and encouraging me every step of the way, to all the husbands and wives who have gone through their own miscarriages and to God for giving me the courage and words to write this book.

Note

Three years ago my book "Marriages and Miscarriages: One Woman's Personal Experience" was published. Over the last three years I have met so many people who have encouraged me and thanked me for writing my story. Now I'm excited to add a new chapter to the book and create an updated edition.

I hope God blesses you as I share my experiences and you read my story.

-- Kathleen

Introduction

Sometimes it isn't easy to understand what your spouse is going through. In the case of the topic of this book, miscarriages, it may be especially difficult for a man to understand what a woman is going through. For the last few years my wife has desired to put down her thoughts about the experiences we had going through three miscarriages.

In reading this book, I believe you will experience sitting down with Kathleen and having a conversation. We pray that hearing what we went through may help you better understand a situation with yourself or others. More importantly, it lets you see how one person thinks and deals with a situation like this.

You will not find this to be a self-help book or scholarly psychological advice. You will find the story of a real person, the experiences of a person I love dearly. She is someone who can sometimes be blunt, sometimes shy, sometimes outgoing, but always sincere.

When Kathleen and I first started dating, we started a tradition. Each time we would leave each other we would pray together. Now, each night when we go to sleep we pray. God, and our personal relationships with Jesus Christ are an important part of what you are about to read. Without Jesus' gift of salvation, without the Holy Spirit's guidance, we would be lost.

We both hope that you benefit from reading about this experience and seeing how one person has dealt with this difficult situation.

--Andrew Smith

(Kathleen's Husband)

Miscarriages

My Story

By Kathleen Smith

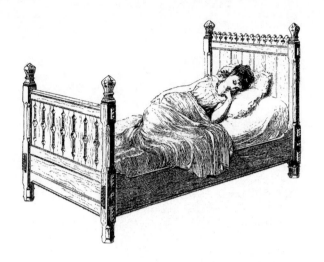

Chapter 1
Having a Miscarriage

When my husband and I were dating, or courting, as he likes to put it, we discussed how many children we would like to have. When he told me he wanted to have ten kids I thought he was kidding so I laughed. He wasn't kidding. I told him I wanted to have three kids. He thought I was kidding so he laughed. I wasn't. So we compromised and agreed on five. All was good or so we thought.

Having a miscarriage is not an easy thing to go through physically or emotionally. I can honestly say it can take a lot out of a woman. I also know that feeling one way about one miscarriage can be totally different than how you feel about another miscarriage. I say this from experience. I personally have had three miscarriages and my emotions were different with all three.

As I was going through what I thought was my first pregnancy, I had to recount my menstrual history with the midwife I was seeing. After this discussion, we both realized that I had previously been pregnant, but had a miscarriage at a very early stage. By then it had no effect on me because I didn't know while it was occurring.

My second miscarriage was more difficult to go through. I was two months along when I lost that baby. I was saddened by it, but I was overcome by the worry I was feeling when I was told I needed to go for some ultrasounds because there was something there and the doctors couldn't figure out what it was. It turned out I needed surgery to have what was left of the baby removed. I was also told it was called a tubular pregnancy.

I was at my eleventh week of my third pregnancy when things started to go poorly. I was so close to the three-month mark when I started to spot. The spotting turned into bleeding. The bleeding turned into my last miscarriage. This was my most difficult miscarriage to go through physically and emotionally.

My husband and I spent that day in the hospital going through the motions. It was draining. When we were finally able to get ready to leave the hospital, I walked over to where my husband was sitting on the hospital bed and as I cried, I told him I was sorry. He asked me why I was sorry. I told him it was because I knew he originally wanted to have ten kids and I could only give him two. I felt like such a failure. He then proceeded to cry himself and told me I was doing a great job with having our kids and that he was very happy with our family. We cried together for a bit.

It took me a very long time to believe that he really was happy with our family just the way it was. Not because I thought he was lying to me since I knew he wasn't lying, but because I couldn't understand how he could be so content with our family knowing he would have liked more children. Thinking back on it, I think it is also because it is a part of his personality to go with the flow of things, so it was easier for him to accept having a smaller family.

That night before we left the hospital, I was told I had to wait for the baby to pass or they would have to take care of it. The next day was Valentine's Day and it was the worst Valentine's Day I ever had. I wasn't feeling good at all. I was waiting for my body to do what it needed to do. That night it happened.

So, the physical pain was over and done with for me. My guess is for other women the physical pain can last longer, especially if they had to have a procedure called a D&C. I am thankful I didn't have to go through that. For me, my physical pain was more than enough for me to deal with and yet I know there are other women out there who have dealt with much more physical pain after a miscarriage.

I also understand that it doesn't matter if you had one miscarriage or five. Each one could very well hurt as much as the last, physically it depends on the woman's body. I also think there is a possibility of none of them hurting. However, I doubt that.

The emotional pain that started that day was going to last me a very long time. It was going to be a pain unlike any other pain that I had ever felt. A pain that only time and God could heal.

Chapter 2
Talking With My Husband

It was so very important for my husband and I to get our feelings out in the open and to say, "I feel this way or that way", and to hear each other out. The worst thing we could have done was to hold anything back from each other. Talking to him. Telling him how I felt about our miscarriages. Leaning on his shoulder. Crying on his shoulder. Holding each other. It was so very important for the two of us to let each other know how we were feeling. Holding anything back could have ruined our marriage and I certainly didn't want that. Talking with each other strengthened our marriage. It brought us so much closer to each other. Finding out how my husband felt about our miscarriages was a big help to me as well.

I don't think people realize this, but husbands also hurt emotionally from a miscarriage. They may not show it, but they are feeling it. Or they show it, but nowhere near as much. Or they show it differently.

My husband needed to cry on my shoulder as much as I needed to cry on his. I held him and loved him as much as he needed to be held and loved, the way he was there for me. I sat and listened to him explain how he felt and hurt just as he listened to me when I needed to talk to him. At times he surprised me with what he had to say, but I am so glad I listened. It didn't matter if our conversations lasted for five minutes or two hours. The point is, we were talking to each other. Letting each other know exactly how we were feeling.

My husband's emotional pains went away a lot fast than mine did. I didn't find that to be fair, but he is a man and I am a woman so I don't think I had all that much of a choice, but if I could have I would have gotten rid of my emotional pains just as fast. I must say I did find it annoying. Even though my husband did feel the emotional pain, he is still a man and didn't feel it anywhere near as long as I did. That is something I had to deal with. However, I didn't stop talking to my husband. Just because his grieving was over, didn't mean mine was.

My grieving wasn't done and I still needed to talk to him. I still need to let him know how I was feeling. In the long run, all these talks with my husband were a huge benefit for me. Why? Because we both needed to know where each other stood with our feelings and that is very important.

In all the conversations I had with my husband, I always made sure I told him how much I loved him and gave him a hug. I always said to him, "thank you for listening to me." Even if it didn't seem to help that much at the time, I realized later that it still helped.

I found that praying with my husband was also a very good thing for me to do. It didn't have to be a long prayer, just something simple. The more I talked with my husband and prayed with him about how I was feeling and about the miscarriages, the closer God put the two of us together. The closer our relationship with each other became and that was and is so very important. I do believe very strongly in this. I believe if I didn't talk with my husband, it could have very easily ruined our relationship with each other and the hurting would have gotten worse. I didn't want that. I kept the communications open with my husband even when it got frustrating because I was still hurting so much and he wasn't any more. His thoughts were different at this point, that's okay. At times I did get very frustrated with him because he wasn't getting it. Unfortunately, I can't say I never got mad at him during a conversation because I did get mad. I didn't want to get mad, but because he sometimes couldn't understand what I was feeling at that time it got to me. I would walk away from him at that point. However, I always went back and talked with him when I needed to.

At times I kept talking until I was able to get out what I was feeling in a way that I found effective enough so that he was able to say to me "okay, I can sort of see your point." He still didn't agree with me, but at least he was able to see my point of view. That was all I wanted at that point.

I didn't give up on talking with my husband because if I did, then there would have been a good chance at us not talking at all and I most certainly didn't want that. That would not have been good. That could have very easily have ruined our marriage, quite possibly to the point of a divorce and I love my husband too much to let that ever happen. I definitely never want that to happen. I didn't want to ruin my marriage just because we stopped talking. In fact, I never ever want to ruin my marriage; therefore I prefer to always talk to my husband. It always makes me feel better afterwards.

Chapter 3
Being Envious

Being envious of other women is not a good thing. I remember after my second miscarriage thinking about my friend a lot. At the time it felt like she was having all these babies, and all I had was my two kids. I kept thinking how it wasn't fair. Why was she getting to have these babies and I had to settle for two? I was dwelling on it so much I was getting depressed. I kept thinking "Why God?" I wasn't concentrating on what I had, on what was right in front of me.

One day while I was doing the laundry, it hit me like a ton of bricks. I was coveting. I wanted what she had. This was not good. I stopped what I was doing immediately and prayed a little prayer. I asked God to forgive me and to allow me to be happy and content with what He gave me. That night I talked with my husband to make sure I was correct with what I thought about what I was feeling. It felt so good to talk with him and to know I was getting on the right track. From that point on, I looked at my kids in a totally different way.

I was able to love my kids even more than I had before and enjoy them more. I embraced them more. I began to be so happy with my family and was very happy and content with what God gave me.

Please don't be envious of other women. Be content with the one child God has given you or the two kids He has given you or however many kids He has given you. They are so special in their own ways and they are YOURS. I learned to never want what another woman has, to be thankful for all that God has given me and I was surprised with the peace that only God could give me and has given me after learning that lesson. I started to love my family in a way I never thought possible.

Let me tell you, being envious can and will take a lot out of you. I did not and do not want that.

Until this day, my friend still has more kids than I do and I am totally okay with that. She is also one of my very closest friends and I have a good time with her every time we get together.

Chapter 4
Being Around Other Pregnant Women

Each time I lost one of my babies, being around other pregnant women was not an easy thing for me to do.

This happened to me with my second and third miscarriage. When I had my second miscarriage a friend of mine was also pregnant. I can't even begin to tell you how difficult it was for me to see her each week at Church. It was a reminder of what I lost. I couldn't look at her for months. It made me want to cry. She finally had her baby, and yes, I couldn't look at her baby either. It was extremely bad. The sadness I felt was so overwhelming.

All I could think to myself was, "it's so unfair". Why did she get to have her baby and mine was taken away? I didn't have an answer then and I don't have one now. Over a period of time, the pain slowly went away and I can honestly tell you that I am still friends with her and I can now have a good time with her and chat. I can even look at her child and talk with her child. I am at peace with it and it's a nice feeling.

When I had my third miscarriage another friend of mine was pregnant, although this time things were different. I didn't know her yet. I know that sounds odd, but all I had to hear was that she was pregnant, and that she was due on the exact day I would have been due. That, for some reason, did me in. The first time I saw her was at a class reunion of my husband's and I made sure to stay away from her as much as possible. She did eventually have her baby and it was on that due date and I was crying.

One day I was kind of forced to have to talk with her. So I did my best to be friendly, but not overly friendly. Here's the kicker! That one conversation turned into a very strong friendship that I didn't expect. She is now one of my dearest and best friends. She is the one I turn to for so many different things to talk about and ask for advice. The baby she had has become very dear to me as well. Now we have an even stronger bond because she too has gone through having miscarriages. I'm not glad that she had those miscarriages. Not at all, but they did help us to understand each other much better than before.

I wonder how many women go through or have gone through what I did. Are they having trouble being around other women who are pregnant after their miscarriages? Especially when it is one of their friends? Do they feel that same emotional hurt? Do they think to themselves "why me and not her"? or do they think "why me?" Are they struggling?

I believe this is a natural feeling, the pain and the hurt. I wanted to cry my heart out and not be anywhere near these women because it reminded me of what I lost. Even after their babies were born, I still felt this way.

Here is the good news. It went away! All of that hurting went away. All the bitterness I had towards these women, it all just vanished. What I needed was time and lots of it. Have you ever heard the saying "time heals all wounds"? As strange as it might sound, it really does. It wasn't just time that healed my emotions though. I also did a lot of talking with my husband, which I have said before.

There was a wedding that I had been looking forward to attending for weeks. Unfortunately, I had my second miscarriage on the same weekend of that wedding and was feeling awful. I didn't know what to do. I was wondering, should I go to the wedding or should I stay home?

I talked with my husband and asked him what he thought. I asked him if he wanted to go or if he wanted to stay home. He didn't care either way. He told me if I wanted to go we could, but he would understand if I wanted to stay home and do nothing. I had to think about this a lot. I wasn't sure if I wanted to be around other people, especially knowing that there would be other women there that were still pregnant. Then I started to think to myself that being around other people might distract me from what I had lost. So I made up my mind, said yes, and went. Bad mistake.

After that wedding's ceremony we were talking with some friends outside the Church and the next thing I knew I couldn't keep the tears back any longer and cried. One of our friends quietly asked me if I had just had a miscarriage. How she knew was beyond me, but she figured it out. She told me how sorry she was to hear that. The reception was no easier for me to deal with.

At the beginning of that reception the first thing I did was to walk over to my Pastor's wife and ask her if we could go somewhere else to talk quickly. She was busy helping out with the food and asked me if it could wait, not knowing what was going on and I said no. We did find a quiet place in the

Church and I then proceeded to tell her that I had lost my baby. We both started to cry together and we talked. She then prayed with me and for me and that helped me get through the rest of that reception. Smiling, talking, trying to laugh that day was not any fun. It wasn't worth going to that wedding for me that day.

Then there was a baby shower and the questions "should I go or should I stay at home? Am I going to be able to have fun or am I going to be miserable? Can I handle it emotionally or not? Am I going to be able to laugh along with the other women? Am I going to be able to see all the cute little baby clothes and toys and what not and be okay with it all?" I had to make the decision whether or not to go. Even though I just had my second miscarriage, I made my decision and I went, only because I thought I had to go. I thought if I didn't go that it would mean I was being rude.

It was a very big mistake for me to go to that baby shower. I was so very miserable. The tears stung my eyes so badly, but I never let them out. I played all the usual games, but didn't have any fun.

I watched as the presents were being opened with this emptiness in my heart. Going to that baby shower was one of the worst decisions I ever made. I was definitely not ready emotionally to be around any one.

34

Chapter 5
The Body Can't Be Controlled

And the LORD God said unto the woman, What is this that thou hast done? And the woman said, The serpent beguiled me, and I did eat. And the LORD God said unto the serpent, Because thou hast done this, thou art cursed above all cattle, and above every beast of the field; upon thy belly shalt thou go, and dust shalt thou eat all the days

of thy life: And I will put enmity
between thee and the woman, and
between thy seed and her seed; it
shall bruise thy head, and thou
shalt bruise his heel. Unto the
woman he said, I will greatly
multiply thy sorrow and thy
conception; in sorrow thou shalt
bring forth children; and thy desire
shall be to thy husband, and he
shall rule over thee.
Genesis 3:13-16

I have been thinking about what we women
have gone through with having these miscarriages
and the more I thought about it the more I realized
there isn't anyway for us to control it.

Women have been having miscarriages for
centuries and there is nothing anyone can do about.
The more I thought about it, the more I started to
ask myself why a woman's body rejects the baby.
Then, I thought about Eve. All was well in the
Garden of Eden until Eve decided to disobey God
and listened to the serpent. As soon as she took of

that forbidden fruit, things started to go downhill for mankind. She and Adam were cast out of the Garden of Eden for their disobedience. After that, they were told they were going to have to work for their food and that it was going to hurt the women every time they gave birth. As years and centuries went by, the human body started to have problems; along with that came a woman's body not being able to have babies or losing the babies. In a way, you could almost consider it a part of the punishment that Eve was given. It is a sad thing to think about one person's sin affecting so many people over such a long period of time.

It isn't like getting the Flu or Strep and going to the Doctors, going through the exam and coming to the conclusion that you have the Flu or Strep and the Doctor gives you medicine to take for ten days and then you're fine again. There is no medicine to prevent a miscarriage. If there were, women would be lining up at the door waiting for that prescription. Women can't help the fact that their bodies might say, "yes" to one baby, "I'll keep you for nine months" and then say to another baby, "no thanks, not you."

Our bodies are difficult to figure out and there isn't a Doctor or Scientist on this planet that's going to be able to tell women "oh well, you had this baby because of such and such," and, "you had this miscarriage or miscarriages for such and such a reason." They don't know why it happens. Yes, a Doctor can run some tests and tell a woman, "your body has this or that", which will make it difficult for her to get pregnant, but I don't think a Doctor can say for sure why a woman's body rejects the baby altogether and has the miscarriage. You could almost consider it a hit or miss.

I think this is something that needs to be accepted, whether we like it or not. Women obviously have no control over their bodies when this happens. We certainly will get very upset and cry and get frustrated and sad. Then we have to go through the waiting process for the emotional part to end, no matter how long that takes, and yeah, it's going to take some time. This is something we have to deal with. We should not get mad at our bodies for what they can't control. We need to go through the process and unfortunately be patient. Being patient with our bodies after going through a miscarriage will not be easy, but I don't think there is any choice.

Chapter 6
Talking or Praying to God

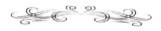

Even more importantly, I needed to talk with God. I needed to pray as often as it took. Obviously God already knew how I felt, but that didn't mean I should stop talking with him, ask Him to give me the strength I needed for each day, for each moment. I still needed to ask God for help with the emotions I was feeling, the hurt. God got me through it. It took some time, but He did. I leaned on God as much as I needed to each day. He was ready and waiting for me to go to Him with open arms.

When I was going through all this, I had to keep reminding myself of this scripture verse:

> **Proverbs 3:5** *Trust in the Lord with all thine heart; and lean not unto thy own understanding.*

This verse was a huge help to me. At the time, I had no idea why God was allowing me to have my miscarriages, but I had to trust that He knew what He was doing.

Another verse that helped me:

> **Psalm 37:4** *Delight thyself also in the Lord, and he shall give thee the desires of thine heart.*

For whatever His reasons were, He wanted me to wait, to be patient even. For all I knew, He could have been testing me for some reason. I did trust in Him and I waited on Him and I know He knew the desires of my heart and in His own time He allowed me to have another baby.

> *Psalm 62:8 Trust in him at all*
> *times; ye people, pour out your*
> *heart before him: God is a refuge*
> *for us*

I think you will find if you open your Bible and start looking through it; you will find many verses having to do with trusting in God especially in the Psalms. I personally like to use the King James Version of the Bible.

I can remember doing a lot of praying. It didn't matter what I was doing, whether it was the dishes, the laundry or just looking out the window, I would start praying and asking God to help me. I would ask, "why me?" I even did it sometimes while I was driving.

I can't tell you that I am happy I had my miscarriages, but what I can tell you is if I hadn't had them, then I wouldn't have the kids I do have and I wouldn't trade my kids in for the world. I love my kids so very much. I can appreciate and love my three kids even more than I ever thought possible because if I hadn't had those miscarriages, then my kids would not be here today with me.

Some woman might be thinking, "Why should I trust in God, He let me lose my baby?" Why not trust in God? Yes, He allows women to lose their babies, but He has his reasons. One way of thinking about it is this. If for whatever reason a wife cannot talk to her husband or a friend then, who can she turn to? God is the only one left. If for whatever reason a woman does not believe in Him, now would be a pretty good time to start. If women seek after God they will be surprised at what will happen. He will help them get through this as long as they let Him.

Chapter 7
Crying

When I was going through my miscarriages, I can remember doing a lot of crying. I couldn't help it. The tough part was when I was in public and I could feel the tears coming. I do not like to cry in public, so I would always do my best to wait till I at least got into my car and then I let the tears go. It didn't necessarily make me feel better all the time, but the tears were there and they needed to get out. I can remember crying and praying at the same time.

Don't be scared to cry. I think it's one of the most important ways for people to get their emotions out. I know it is for me. Quite possibly, it is the only way to get emotions out at times. I was very surprised to find out how many tears I actually had in my eyes. Just when I thought I couldn't possibly cry any more, it started all over again.

One way I look at it is if God didn't want us to cry then he wouldn't have given us tears. Crying can be a very powerful tool when you've had a miscarriage. Crying is not a sign of weakness, quite the opposite. How often do women or girls cry because they are so frustrated over something that they can't take any more and they start to cry? A lot. How do they feel afterwards? They feel some relief; it may not be a lot, but it's just enough for them to be able to get through whatever it is they are going through. It's pretty much the same with a miscarriage. I got so frustrated because I didn't know why it happened to me and all I could do was cry. Getting the hurt and frustrations out with my crying helped to strengthen me. It didn't make me weak at all. I just let myself go. I was okay after that.

As strange as this may sound after all these years, after my last miscarriage sometimes I still get tears in my eyes when I talk about it with my friend, or anyone. Just explaining how I felt back then with what I was going through, it brings tears to my eyes.

My friend's experience was different then mine because she was able to have closure and I didn't. Actually, I think that made a big difference. Even though both of our babies passed through our bodies the way they were supposed to, she was able to see hers and know it was all done. Because I got sick I didn't get to see my baby and did not get that closure. So I had to deal with it the best I could.

After all these years, I still sometimes find it hard to talk with other people about my miscarriages and I still at times feel those tears swelling up in my eyes. It isn't because I still hurt. It's because of all I went through. It isn't a bad thing either. It's me being a woman and a mother remembering, but after all the years that have passed they aren't painful tears. They are the remembering tears.

I don't ever want to forget that I lost my babies. They are a reminder of what God has taken away and what he has given to me. The tears come and go. I'm not scared of them, there's no need for me to be scared of them because those particular tears only last for about a minute. I don't let the tears out; I end up actually choking on them myself because I don't like to cry in front of people and I personally don't think the people would understand. I try my best not to let people notice that it's happening.

Chapter 8
Why Me?

About a year ago I got curious about what questions woman might have about miscarriages. So I went on my book's Facebook page and I asked people what kind of questions they might have. I thought if people had any questions about miscarriages, how women deal with them and the emotions that go with miscarriages maybe I could help. Maybe I could answer those questions the best way possible that I know. The only question I was asked is "Why Me?"

I started to think about that question and thought "Wow, that's a really good question." I also realized that's a BIG question. That's one loaded question and how am I going to answer it. The next thing I know I have all these thoughts going through my mind like crazy and I thought, "Really Lord, what? Another book or do I just write down my answer and see what happens?" I thought, "I can't write another book!" "I'm not a writer." Then I read a tweet on Twitter that was directed to me that said, "you need to keep writing, your journey is not done." All I could think was "Yeah, Right. My journey is done." I wrote the first edition of this book and as far as I know it's helping some women, which I am totally grateful for. Problem is these thoughts about "Why Me?" wouldn't leave my head. So here I am giving it all up to God and asking Him for the help only He can give me. He's allowing all these thoughts to enter into my mind and if I don't get them down they're going to drive me crazy.

So Here I am trying my best to answer the

question "Why Me?"

"Why Me?" Seems to be the biggest question I hear from most women when it comes to having a miscarriage. "Why Me Lord? Why not some other women?" The thing is I don't think I can give you a very good answer. I can try, but I only know my own experiences when it comes to miscarriages. Yeah, I asked that very questions myself "Why Me? Why did I have to have my miscarriages?" Now, for me personally I think the reason why God allowed me to have my miscarriages is so that I would look towards Him for support and strength. For me it was kind of like "well, what's the right thing to do?" Walk away from God and try my best to get through my miscarriages on my own or say "Okay God I can't do this on my own, it hurts way to much, please help me" Deep down in my heart I knew I needed God's help. Without Him my emotional hurt would just get worse. I really believe God allowed me to have my miscarriages so I would allow my relationship with him to grow and become stronger.

I can't even count the amount of times I would

ask God "Why me?" but with each of my three miscarriages I would ask that very question. I believe it was my third and last miscarriage that really had me asking that question "Why Me?" That third and last time is also the one that hurt me the most emotionally. The one where I really needed to look towards God and say, "Help. Please. I can't do this on my own".

You know it's kind of amazing how God can give an experience like a miscarriage to strengthen a person. It didn't just happen overnight. Each time my emotions got the better of me I would turn to God ask for help, lean on him and say "I can't do this." Then it always felt like God was saying back to me "Yes, you can. Let me carry you through this and you will get through it."

What I didn't realize right away is what God was also doing by letting me have my three miscarriages; He was using them to make me talk with my husband more. It was like God was saying, "okay, I gave you this situation now talk with your husband and see what happens." So I did. I talked with my husband. Then I talked some more and as

56

time went on we talked even more and prayed together. Our marriage became stronger and stronger.

I think the other reason why God allowed me to have my three miscarriages is so that I could become a voice for other women who struggle emotionally from miscarriages too. He has allowed me to become very outspoken about it. Which I can tell you is a very far cry from the way I was about miscarriages when they were actually happening to me. When I was going through my last miscarriage, I didn't want to talk to anyone about it. I would just assume change the topic. I couldn't even look people in the eyes when the topic "miscarriage" came up. I didn't want them to know I went through it.

Now I realize what the Lord has done in my life. He has given me this voice to be bold and speak out about miscarriages. To let other women know they aren't alone. That it's okay to be emotional about it. It's ok to cry about it. It's okay to talk about. Now it seems like I'm almost bursting at the seams wanting to let people know, "hey, miscarriages happen." It's nothing to be embarrassed about. It is something women need plenty of support with, especially from their husbands. It's more important that they trust in God.

Now the question is how do I answer "Why Me?" for other women. Honestly I don't know if I can. Each woman is different. What I do think is after asking that question "Why Me?" women then need to start listening to God for that answer. He's really the only one who has that answer or answers. He is the one who allows women to have their miscarriages so it makes sense that God is the one they should be asking that question and then seeking him for the answer. I don't know how long it's going to take for that answer. Maybe he has a ministry for each woman who goes through having miscarriages. Maybe He wants to see if these women will go to Him and lean on Him. Woman need to talk and pray to Him. Maybe He wants to see their reactions. There are way too many maybes to this question "Why Me?" I think it's an individual question and answer.

I do believe though if women do turn to God when they ask "Why Me?" He will in time give them an answer. They need to listen though and accept whatever His answer maybe. Once women get their answers there can be a peace about it.

I really wish I could give you a better answer than what I just did, but it seems like such a personal question that it really needs to be between a woman and God.

I would also like to add that everything I said above I believe can and should be applied by women who for whatever reason can't have any children. There is a reason to that "Why Me?" for them too. All women need to be willing to listen to God, trust in Him and do His will for their lives. He will eventually give that much needed answer.

Chapter 9
Turning To God

The way I saw it was, I had two choices: I could have either turned away from God and said: "You don't care about me. You took my babies from me, why should I have anything to do with you?" Or I could have turned to God and strengthened my relationship with Him. I could have leaned on Him for all the support I needed and let Him guide me through my miscarriages. Reading the Bible and praying, a lot, was also something I could have done, and did.

I chose to turn to God and I know that was the right decision. Yes, I asked Him so many times, "why me? Why not some other woman?" Believe it or not, having my miscarriages brought me closer to God. It made me pray more. It made me read His Word more. It definitely strengthened my relationship with God.

My husband is always telling me, "God will not give you any more than what you can deal with." I guess God thought I could deal with my three miscarriages better than some other women could. I wouldn't be surprised if he thought the same about other women as well who have gone through having a miscarriage. Again, I can't tell you why He let me go through my miscarriages; it is possible that He did it to test me and to see if I would actually go towards Him and lean on Him or if I would turn my back on Him. He did, however, get me through them all with my husband. It did take quite a while for me to get through them emotionally, but He most definitely did get me through it all. I know He can do the same for other women. He can and will get other husbands and wives through this together as He did for my husband and me. We had to let God work in and through the two of us as a couple and, when needed, as individuals. Other couples can do this too.

I didn't give up on God because He never gave up on me or us as a couple. He was always on my side; I just needed to trust in Him. I know that is a big word: "TRUST," but in the end it was all worth it and I did become happy again and content. With all things, it takes time. Believe it or not, the emotional pain I was feeling went away with God's help.

Chapter 10
I Answer, "I'm Okay"

I found after having my miscarriages, my friends would come up to me and they would all ask the same question, "Are you okay?" My first response to that was: "yes, I'm okay" or "I'm fine," but in reality I wasn't okay or fine. What I wanted to do was shout out, "no, I'm not okay!" I wanted to tell them how much I was hurting, but because some of them have never experienced a miscarriage themselves they would not have understood. I wasn't even ready to speak to those that did understand.

There was almost an awkwardness about the question because some of my friends didn't know what else to say to me in the beginning. They wanted to help, but there wasn't anything they could do for me. They thought they should be talking with me about it or maybe even giving me a hug because they didn't get it. I did accept the hugs; I didn't want to, but didn't want to be rude either.

There was a point when my friends and family members would call me to see how I was doing. Every time the phone rang I thought to myself, "not again." I didn't want to answer the phone and talk to any one, so I used to let the answering machine pick up. Sometimes I listened to what they said and sometimes I left the room before they had the chance to even leave the message.

My friends and family needed to understand that they needed to give me some time and space to deal with my loss and eventually they got the message and didn't talk to me about it.

The hardest part, though, for me at that particular time of my life was when I was going through my second miscarriage. My friend was pregnant with her first and all was going well for her, but not me. I had such a hard time being around her. I avoided her like a plague. I couldn't be in the same room with her and, when that couldn't be avoided, I just didn't look at her in that room. Whether she was uncomfortable around me at that time or not, I don't know. There was no way for her to be able to sympathize with me since she never had a miscarriage of her own. I didn't talk to her for months; in fact, I didn't start talking with her until sometime after her baby was born.

Whether she realized what was going on or not, I have no idea. It was something I had to deal with and I saw no reason to clue her in on what was happening. I think that maybe for some women the opposite can happen and maybe the women who are still pregnant might feel awkward around their friends who have had the miscarriage and won't talk to them. Either way, I think only time can heal those wounds. I experienced this myself; I no longer feel like avoiding people who I previously felt uncomfortable around.

I have found over the years, whether talking with friends that I met after I had my miscarriages and had no idea that I had them, or talking with people in general about having families, eventually these two questions would always come up. I would either be asked, "do you wish you had had more children? Or "do you regret not having any more children?" I always answer the same way. "Yes, sometimes I wish I had more", or "Yes, sometimes I regret not having any more." I usually wait a minute, debating whether or not I should say anything about my miscarriages and then I decide to say something, figuring it can't hurt. I end up telling the people that, technically, I have been pregnant six times. The response is usually the same. They give me a bit of a shocked look and don't know what to say, so they generally say: "Oh."

Things always feel a bit awkward after that. I don't know why. People react to that one word "miscarriage" like it's a curse or a disease or a sin. In reality, it is none of the above. Unfortunately, though, it is something that does happen and it happens a lot. There is nothing to be embarrassed about either. It's something that I don't mind talking about.

At times, it does bother me when I get that look of surprise from people who find out for the first time that I had three miscarriages and other times I sort of feel like just hiding under a rock or running away so I don't have to deal with it, but it is something that needs to be dealt with and people need to understand that it is a painful topic at times. One that I am willing to talk about and answer questions if I have the answers. Although I must say it would be nice just once not to get that reaction from people, mainly women, when they find out that I did indeed have three miscarriages.

Chapter 11
Wondering

I can remember after I had my kids wondering what my last baby that I lost would have looked like. Would he or she have had blond hair or brown? Blue, green or brown eyes? I kept dwelling on it. I was having a lot of trouble getting it off my mind.

One day, as I was thinking about it, I all of a sudden looked at my kids and started thinking to myself, "What am I thinking?" Here sitting in front of me are three wonderful kids that God has given me that I love with all my heart and here I am neglecting them with my thoughts about a baby that isn't even here. I felt so bad! I started to realize that I needed to stop thinking about what I lost and start concentrating on what was right in front of me. I needed to love the kids that God gave me. I immediately stopped what I was doing and prayed. I asked God to forgive me and to allow me to love the kids that I have.

From that point on, I concentrated on my kids. I didn't forget that I lost my other babies and I still haven't forgotten about that, but I realized that dwelling on what I don't have, instead of loving what I do have, was wrong of me. Yes, I will always remember that I lost three of my babies, but that is not what I need to focus on. I need to focus on what God has given me.

I can't help but wonder how many women dwell on the babies that they have lost to miscarriages rather than looking at the kids they have that are right in front of them as well. I don't think it's totally wrong to wonder about what the baby or babies would have looked like, but if it's going to take over their thoughts completely, then that I think is bad.

It's something that I think mom's can even talk about with their kids as they grow up because I think it's something that their kids should know. I think it's healthy for moms to talk with their kids about their miscarriages. I think it's good for moms to share their thoughts with their kids and let them, in return, share their thoughts. Moms might be surprised at what their kids or kid has to say. I'm not saying that moms have to do this. I am just making a suggestion to them.

I have talked with my kids about my miscarriages. They have asked me what would have happened if I didn't have those miscarriages. I told them flat-out if I had those babies, then they wouldn't be here now and I wouldn't trade them in for anything.

I personally think it's important to be open and honest with kids about miscarriages, but without too many details. I think kids can understand only so much and so the details that are given to them should only be so much and, at the same time, I think the kids should know that this does happen. However, keep in mind that little kids and teenagers have different mentality levels so, it would be best to only tell your little child just so much. There is more that can be elaborated on with teens to an extent. Volunteering the information to the teens is not necessary, but if he or she asks questions, then I would answer them. My guess is it will most likely be the teen girl to ask the questions. However, if a mom has a preteen or teen son, don't be surprised if he asks questions about the miscarriage too.

Chapter 12
No Children

Even though I am writing about what it's like to go through having a miscarriage or multiple miscarriages and still having kids, I feel it is also important to remember there are also lots of women who have had either one miscarriage or many miscarriages and don't have any children at all. I believe that some of the same principles are applied to them as to women with kids and have had miscarriages.

I do think it's very important for women with no kids and have had miscarriages to still talk with their husbands and let their feelings out and let their husbands talk to them too, not holding anything back from each other. I believe the only thing you're going to do is hurt each other and your marriage if you don't talk with each other.

I also believe those women can look towards God. He has His reasons for allowing husbands and wives to not have any kids at all, just as He allows other couples to have only one or others to have more. We don't know God's reasons, but we have to trust in Him. I truly believe women who have had one miscarriage after another and have no children especially need to turn God for support. Yeah He's allowing this to happen and yeah, I have no idea why, but there's that trust issue again. I think they just have to do it.

I can very easily say to a woman who has had a miscarriage and can't have any kids for whatever reason, "I'm sorry," but what good is that going to do her? It's like when one woman who has never had a miscarriage and has several kids, tells another woman, who has had a miscarriage and does have at least one kid that she's sorry. Yeah, she means it, but she has absolutely no idea what this other woman is going through. It's the same thing. I have absolutely no idea what women are going through who have had one miscarriage after another and have no kids. I do feel bad for them, but saying "I'm sorry" doesn't seem to cut it.

I know God has His reasons, as He does for everything He lets happen to people, but that doesn't mean I understand. Why let this couple have ten, another couple five, and yet another couple to just have one and then the last couple none? Doesn't seem fair, does it?

I do know women who have tried to have babies and they can't for one reason or for another. I think these women would make great moms. I think, and I could be wrong, but I think that women who have had at least one miscarriage and can't have kids for whatever reason or who have never had a miscarriage and can't get pregnant at all need to trust in God and say, "okay, in His time if He wants me to ever have a child, then He will allow and bless me with a child", otherwise, I think they need to be content with the life God has given them.

It may not always be easy, but that is when I think they need to lean on God and trust Him. Yeah I know easy for me to say, I have kids, but at the same time I feel silly saying to them "I'm sorry." I do feel bad that they can't have kids, but God does have something for those women, even if it's not motherhood. I hope I don't get any women mad or upset over saying this. That is not my intention at all. I think it would be great if God allowed those women to have at least one kid some day.

In the meantime, I hope and pray that women who have had miscarriages and cannot, for whatever reason, have a baby or maybe can't get pregnant at all, I hope they will always remember to talk with their husband and get their feelings out and, even more importantly, I hope they will always turn to God and ask Him to help them get through this. Like I said, I have absolutely no idea how they feel about this, but at the same time I do think it is important for other women to realize that even though they have had at least one miscarriage and have kids, there are still women who have had at least one miscarriage and can't have any kids at all that are hurting emotionally too.

Chapter 13
Content

I know I have spoken a little about this before, but I am finding there is more to say-being content. Sometimes the word content sounds so strong and other times you don't give it another thought. A while ago, I started to think about that word. I don't know if my pastor talked about it in one of his messages or if God was speaking to my heart or what, but there it was. It made me think about my family and what the word content means in the dictionary and what verses use it in the Bible.

The first thing I realized was how content I am with my kids. I started to think about them and how many I have and I realized how happy I am with my family. Yes, sometimes I wish I had more kids, but I know I had the amount of kids that God wanted me to have and that helps me to be content.

The first thing I looked up was the definition of the word content in the dictionary. I learned that content is defined as being happy enough with what one has and not desiring something more or different.

After looking up the word content in the dictionary, I then proceeded to see what the Bible had. I've listed some of the verses that stood out to me.

> **Philippians 4:11** *Not that I speak in respect of want : for I have learned, in whatsoever state I am , therewith to be content.*
>
> **I Timothy 6:6** *But godliness with*

contentment is great gain.

Hebrews 13:5 *Let your
conversation be without
covetousness; and be content with
such things as ye have: for he hath
said, I will never leave thee, nor
forsake thee.*

I do believe it's important for women to be content and satisfied with the amount of kids that God has given them, whether it be one, two, three, or whatever the number. Be content. Be happy. Be satisfied. I know that God has given me the amount of kids that He knows I can handle.

If women are not content with what God has given them, then how can they ever be happy? The two go together. Content, such a strong word. I wonder if women are content with their families? If not, maybe that is something they should start praying about and asking God to give them peace and contentment. It will make their lives much happier. I think it will help them to be able to move on after their miscarriages and with their lives and families. I hope they remember to always love their families.

Chapter 14
Memories

As I write about what its like to go through having a miscarriage or multiple miscarriages, I have found it to bring back memories that I thought were hidden somewhere deep in the back of my mind. A place where I thought I would never go to again. I had all these memories tucked away quite nicely, so as to not think about them any more, but now I'm glad that I do remember, for it has made me realize so many different things about me that I didn't know happened. I didn't see what was going on at the time, but am so grateful that it all happened.

> *I can remember after my first miscarriage thinking, "huh, so I had a miscarriage."*

> *I can remember after my second miscarriage getting ready for surgery and not knowing what the outcome was going to be or if I would ever be able to have any more babies and crying so much and being so fearful.*

> *I can remember attending a wedding the weekend we found out about my second miscarriage. My husband told me we didn't have to go, but I thought being around other people would help me. It didn't. Just made it worse.*

> *I can remember getting together with my husband and many people from*

the school he graduated from getting
together for a Christmas party one
year. I was very close to what would
have been the due date for my second
baby, had I not had the miscarriage. I
remember I was sitting on a bench
and one of my husband's friend's
futher asked me how I was and
wanted to know when I was going to
give my husband a son. I can
remember looking at this man shaking
my head back and forth and telling
him "I don't know." The tears were
stinging my eyes at this point, but I
refused to let this man see me cry. He
eventually walked away and I turned
to a friend and asked her to walk me
to the bathroom so I could cry. I could
barely keep myself together until we
got to the bathroom. Once there, the
tears just wouldn't stop.

I can remember my third and last miscarriage, thinking, "not again!"

I can remember going through all the pain waiting for the baby to pass as I was sick to my stomach and not getting the closure I needed to be able to say good-bye to my baby.

I can remember all the shed tears that never seemed to stop.

I can remember seeing all the pregnant women around me and wishing they would go away.

I can remember seeing all the babies surrounding me and thinking how it wasn't fair.

I can remember talking with my husband until there was nothing more to say and being held by him when words could do nothing and his

*arms around me could do something
even if it was the tiniest bit of
something.*

*I can remember hearing my husband
tell me countless times "I love you
and I'm thankful for the family God
has given us."*

*I can remember praying and praying
and praying.*

*I can remember praying and crying
and asking God, "why me? Why not
someone else?"*

*I can remember leaning on my
husband's shoulders and God's
shoulders countless times.*

Throughout all of this, I knew my relationship with my husband and with God was getting stronger because I was going to both of them and talking with both of them and crying to both of them. What I didn't realize at the time was how close my miscarriages were making my marriage and my relationship with God. I knew I had two choices. Either lean on my husband's shoulders and talk with him and do the same with God or turn my back on both of them and try to get through my miscarriages on my own. I chose to go with my husband and God because I knew there was no way I could get through it by myself. I needed them both so very much.

I'm not thankful for my miscarriages, but I am very thankful that they made my marriage stronger. I am glad they made me go towards God rather than against him. I do think that in a way my miscarriages made me a stronger woman. They made me lean on my husband to the point where I knew I had to talk with him, even if the conversation went nowhere. I was still talking with my husband and loving him more than I ever thought possible. The miscarriages made me look into God's word, the Bible, and see what was there for me. They made me pray so much and ask God for the help only He could give me.

My miscarriages made me even more grateful for the kids that I do have that God was gracious enough to give me. They made me love my kids more than I ever thought possible. Do my kids frustrate me at times? Yes, but I still love them unconditionally.

Chapter 15
I've Become a Writer

In the first edition of this book I wrote about how I wasn't a writer. At the time that was so true. I really had no idea what I was doing. I only knew I had to share my experiences with others. I had a story to tell and I wanted to get it written down. So I did.

Since then I have been doing more writing and

somehow I have become a writer. At least I think so. Since then I have been able to write about how I feel about all sorts of different things. So I went from not being a writer to being a writer and a blogger!

So it's been about three years now since the first edition of my book was printed and publish. I learned some stuff about other women and miscarriages. I learned that there are other women out there who felt the same emotions that I did. I learned that sharing my experiences in my book really did help other women.

I have felt very thankful over the last couple of years to know that my book has indeed helped other women. Whenever I get an email from one of my readers telling me that my book helped them, it is always an overwhelming feeling. It's like "wow!" what I wrote really helped someone else get through her miscarriage. That truly is an amazing feeling. That was the biggest reason for me to write my book.

I hope what I have written will be able to help

more husbands and wives, as a couple, and as individuals to get through the emotional pain of the miscarriage or miscarriages. I hope what I have written will help women who have had miscarriages to realize they need to talk with their husbands and they need to pray and talk with God. These are two very powerful resources to turn to; One greater than the other and both waiting to listen.

I pray that God will use what I have to say and have written to help other women who have gone through what I have gone through or if they are still going through it. I can't help but wonder how many women in this world have gone through at least one miscarriage and have felt the emotional pain I have gone through and struggled with it and are still struggling with it. Keeping their feelings all bottled up inside is not so good.

I pray that if any of these women are still hurting and have no one to talk with, that I could be of some help. I pray that God will use what I have written to help these women, whether it be praying for them or conversing through email. Yes,

I said email. I am more than willing to email with other women who are going through or have gone through a miscarriage and are struggling emotionally. It's a hard thing to go through and no women should have to do it alone. I am adding my email address to what I have written and if there are any women out there who are reading this and have had at least one miscarriage and are hurting emotionally, I hope and pray they will **email** me and maybe I can help them. Maybe there are questions that I can answer. Even if all they ask for is for me to pray for them, I most certainly can do that.

Contact Information

I have really enjoyed putting my experiences into this book. I hope you have enjoyed reading it. The last two chapters gave me the greatest joy in the process.

If you would like to contact me, would like prayer, or to share a need, email me at **katandsmith@gmail.com**

Since publishing the first edition of this book I have become really involved in social media. You can find me talking with other independent authors and with readers on Facebook, LinkedIn, Twitter (@srkbear) and Google+.

You can also read my blog "#HeyYou" and other resources at http://kathleensmith.org

Psalm 139

O lord, thou hast searched me,
> and known me.

Thou knowest my downsitting and mine uprising,
> thou understandest my thought afar off.

Thou compassest my path
> and my lying down,
> and art acquainted with all my ways.

For there is not a word in my tongue, but, lo, O LORD,
> thou knowest it altogether.

Thou hast beset me behind and before,
> and laid thine hand upon me.

Such knowledge is too wonderful for me;
> it is high, I cannot attain unto it.

Whither shall I go from thy spirit?
> or whither shall I flee from thy presence?

If I ascend up into heaven, thou art there:
> if I make my bed in hell, behold, thou art there.

If I take the wings of the morning,
> and dwell in the uttermost parts of the sea;

Even there shall thy hand lead me,
> and thy right hand shall hold me.

If I say, Surely the darkness shall cover me;
> even the night shall be light about me.

Yea, the darkness hideth not from thee;

      but the night shineth as the day:

      the darkness and the light are both alike to thee.

For thou hast possessed my reins:

      thou hast covered me in my mother's womb.

I will praise thee; for I am fearfully and wonderfully made:

      marvellous are thy works;

      and that my soul knoweth right well.

My substance was not hid from thee,

      when I was made in secret,

      and curiously wrought in the lowest parts of the earth.

Thine eyes did see my substance, yet being unperfect;

      and in thy book all my members were written,

      which in continuance were fashioned,

      when as yet there was none of them.

How precious also are thy thoughts unto me, O God!

      how great is the sum of them!

If I should count them, they are more in number than the sand:

      when I awake, I am still with thee.

Surely thou wilt slay the wicked,

      O God: depart from me therefore, ye bloody men.

For they speak against thee wickedly,

      and thine enemies take thy name in vain.

Do not I hate them, O LORD, that hate thee?

and am not I grieved with those that rise up against thee?

I hate them with perfect hatred:

I count them mine enemies.

Search me, O God, and know my heart:

try me, and know my thoughts:

And see if there be any wicked way in me,

and lead me in the way everlasting.

57835325R00060

Made in the USA
San Bernardino, CA
23 November 2017